How to Analyze People

A Total Guide to Analyzing People and Body Language

Table Of Contents

Introduction

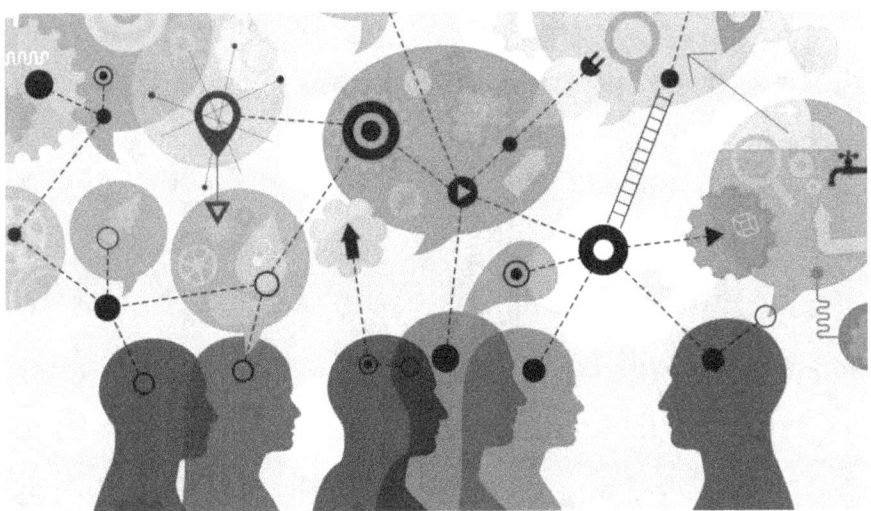

There are times when you wish you were able to read minds; times when one would give anything to know why someone is doing what they are doing and also times when someone wishes that they could hide their feeling to prevent other people from finding out what is in their hearts, or at least make it difficult for them to know what's in his/ her heart. This might come naturally to others, but to most of us, it is a skill that you actually have to learn and practice until you have mastered it. It does not matter at what level or stage of life you are; you can achieve it. This is the purpose of this book. The book is aimed at showing the reader how to analyze people's minds or hide from people what is going on in theirs. If the above are your desires, put your trust in this book, it will show you just how to go about achieving them.

The book looks at different ways in which you can teach yourself to read people using whatever methods the person will be unknowingly showing, and there are many of those methods. It goes on to explain what the person desiring the human analysis ability should look for to be successful in becoming a masterful analyst. Here are many things, many cues to look for in human analysis but if you do not know about them, you won't even notice them and with that failure to notice them goes any chance of analyzing them. Through reading this book, you will move anyone from being someone who knows an insignificant little or maybe even nothing about human behavior; to someone who wields a lot of power through knowing a great deal more than most. You will not regret reading it.

Enjoy the reading!

Chapter 1: Methods and techniques to analyze people effectively

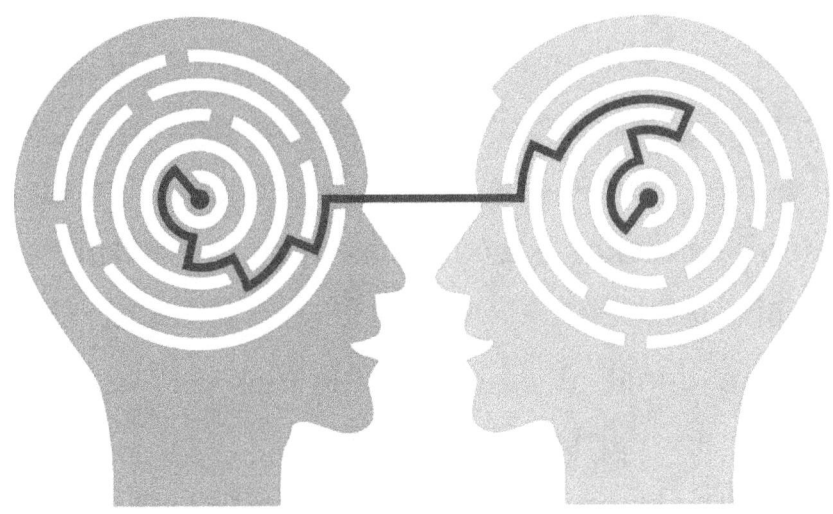

Analyzing people is not something you just get into without carefully thinking about it; on the contrary, you come up with plans and ways on how to perform it. For one, you cannot analyze something you know nothing about, and one good way of knowing about something is reading it, not about it. That having been said, you need to read people to be able to analyze them, in fact, reading is an important part of the analysis. The following methods and techniques will set you up on a path to successfully analyze people.

Get to know yourself

The very first thing you have to achieve before you are able to analyze people is the ability to analyze yourself, the analyst. There are things that you should know about yourself and while striving to do that, you approach your objective. Ask yourself some important questions and give truthful answers to these questions: What is your objective in analyzing the people, or the person you intend to analyze? Are there any emotional attachments between you and your subject of analysis? If there are any, can you trust yourself to be impartial in your analysis? You have to keep from biased analyses because nothing ever comes out of them but the exercise in futility. If you are not going to be able to detach yourself from the subject, waste no more of your precious time.

Observe carefully

If you settled upon being a good analyst, then you need to possess not only good, but exceptional observation skills. The difference between a very good analyst and the general public is that a very good analyst never misses a clue. Where most people fail to see a set of footprints as anything other than footprints, you should see far beyond that. What others might consider too trivial to make any difference, an analyst puts into consideration and finds the details that bring up something which might surprise most. Do not ever get tired of checking and rechecking your cues and findings, and always make sure to take note of anything that means everything you may find. Do not leave stones unturned in your hunt for detail. The right conclusions depend just on that.

Practice persistently

The adage 'Practice makes perfect' might have now turned into a cliché, but it is as true now as it was way back when; maybe it is particularly important these days taking into account the fast life we live, which makes practicing seem a time wasting activity. There are very few things same effective as practicing to make people good at what they want to do. Practice, practice and practice more and soon enough you will find it coming more and more naturally to you. Even when at first it appears as if you are not making any progress in your ability to analyze people, keep on doing it and soon you will find yourself getting better until you are the next Sherlock Holmes; well, maybe not so great but surely somewhere there. Do not only practice, but do it persistently. Draw blood and tears, you **can be sure** in the end: they will be tears of joy born out of your success as the analyst. Yes, it is not done in a day but you will get there with enough practice.

Believe in yourself

Belief in yourself is just one thing you should never take for granted. This simple feeling gives you wings and teaches you to fly. The Wright brothers did it and gave the world the ability to fly. If you believe you are a good analyst of human behavior, this leads to confidence in your work and the beauty of confidence is not something that you just decide you want to have and it comes. No! It is a belief, a conviction that is deeply entrenched in your subconscious, and while you are coming upstairs in your learning how to analyze people, you find yourself growing in confidence and thereby believing in your analyzing prowess more and more. Knowledge and ability are among the things which boost belief in oneself, and getting these qualities sets you on the road to successful human analyses. As you get to know your work better and continue to practice meticulous observation, you are getting comprehension both about yourself as the analyst and about the subject of analysis. That certainly helps to boost your confidence and self-esteem levels. As long as you practice analyzing people and hit closer home with each strike, your ability to handle the analyses is getting stronger, and with it belief in yourself. You are ready.

Focus on the actual subject

There are many occasions when analysts fail to do their work properly, because they fail to separate issues. This problem is too common and has to be dealt with effectively. Whenever you are analyzing a subject, be sure you are analyzing the person under analysis. It means you should make sure that you do not make conclusions about the current subject based on something you discovered in someone else. If you are still hung up on someone else in such a way that you compromise the integrity of your current analysis, then it is not going to be successful. You should start analyzing a new subject with a clean slate so that you do not mix up issues. There is no room for generalizations or stereotyping in a human analysis, let every subject stand on their own. No ghosts from the past or zombies in the future.

Use logic in making conclusions

Logical thinking is an art not common to everyone. You certainly have to master this to a well above average level for you to become an effectual human behavior analyst. The art of logical thinking involves your use of correct values to reason out whatever is at hand. This is an essential exercise to go through before you can safely determine that you have analyzed a subject. Many times people arrive at conclusions about something without working out the situation effectively, and usually it is catastrophic. It is, therefore, crucial that as you do your analyses of people, you use as much logic as you possibly can, in order to arrive at the best conclusions about your subject of analysis. This step requires practicing with as much patience as you can master, because rushing through it will most likely give you the incorrect results and your speed won't help you in anything. It works with the next point.

Give it time

Success rarely, if ever, comes out of rushing through something. Take as much time as you can, because analyzing is certainly not something to do in haste. You will inevitably leave important details out and that won't do. Good analysts do not leave important details, because any detail, no matter how small and seemly unessential, is important and should be treated that way. Even after you have collected all points you think are necessary and you have recorded all available signs, careful thinking about the evidence of what you have and considering the connotations and meanings are of paramount importance. Go through this as painstakingly as you possibly can. That is where the real results lie and you cannot afford to miss that. If you have taken so much time to observe, why ruin a good introduction by concluding shoddily? Slowly but surely is the way to go.

Following the above methods and techniques to analyzing people gets you in the right way and in no time you might just become one of the biggest brains in a human analysis. Remember that if you really want to be an effective human analyst, then you have to follow through with each of the above steps as religiously as you can. These steps will be the determining factor, whether you will be a human analyst of noteworthy ability or just one of those trying their luck. Go for it with all you have, and your success is certain. Avoid short-cuts to success.

Chapter 2: The Human Psychology Concept

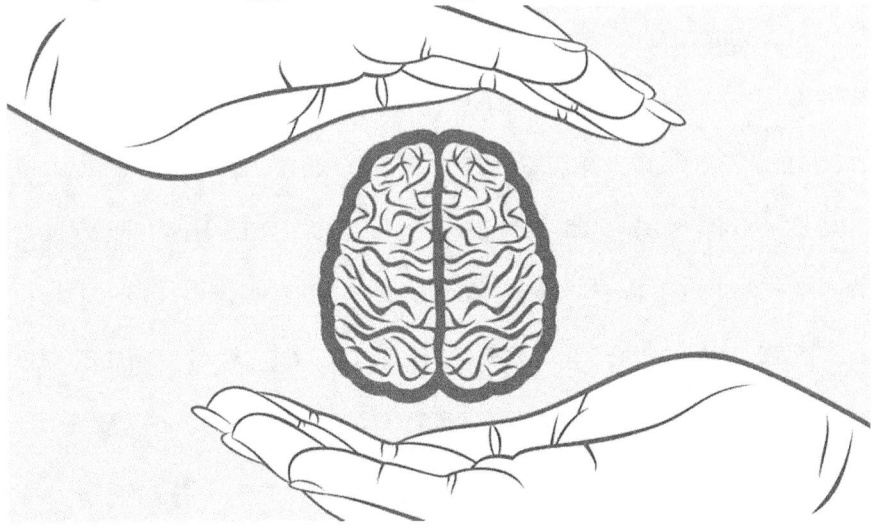

There is something in us that makes us do what we do in the manner we do. It is, as a result, necessary that before you put your money on it, find out some other causative factors about your subject that might have made them behave in a way you consider out of the ordinary. There may be some temporary things in someone's life that might throw an analyst completely off-course.

Cultural differences – In many instances, we tend to label other people in one way or the other because they appear different from us. This mainly happens when we fail to put cultural differences into consideration. I have heard that women from Norway are more assertive than women from most countries as they are the ones who approach men to ask for dates. You have to agree with me that people from most parts of the world, if scrutinizing such a woman for the purpose of analyzing, might be tempted to think the woman as too forward. But to the woman in question that is an ordinary thing to do. On the same note, you cannot go around labeling people as being uneducated because they cannot pronounce certain words 'correctly'. Culture has such a sound grasp on most people that the grip is not easy to separate from. As you try to analyze someone, make sure you know about such things, to ensure that your observations indicate what is the real truth behind the actions; and not an illusion of your own thoughts.

Background – Our backgrounds are as diverse as the peoples of the world. As a result, someone's background can make them send indicators that might end up being misinterpreted. Looking into someone's background can help the analyst in analyzing the subject. Some might not be obvious, but there is something that most of us do because we were influenced thus by our background. For some, shaking off that chip on the shoulder might be difficult than most, and so they carry it around for the longest while. Someone who was bullied as a child might end up hiding behind appearing macho or taking up the bad boy/ bad girl image. This is not the real person inside, but it is merely a veneer that this person is using as protection from the world. In some cultures, wearing a very short dress is just fashion, if that person does that in a different culture, however, she might be regarded as loose and her dressing as a means to attract male attention. It is necessary for you, therefore, to get to the roots of that behavior before making wrong deductions.

Motivation – According to the principle of motivation, unsatisfied needs are our greatest motivators. If you have a strong enough need to satisfy, you might get into all things you may or may not enjoy doing just to enable you to meet the need. If, for instance, you do not have a home for your family, that becomes what motivates you into working hard, maybe even too hard that your body starts to suffer through the hard work. But because you have to satisfy your need, you put your body through rough times so that you buy or build a house for your family. It is, therefore, one of your prerogatives as a human behavior analyst to make sure that you know what your subject's motivation is before you go on to write your findings in stone. When the motivation is strong enough, most people would throw caution to the wind, and even ditch their own principles because they are motivated to react in a particular way. A woman might have been raised to shun prostitution and is principled to believe prostitution is wrong, but an unfortunate financial situation might motivate her to do just what she shuns.

Personality type – There are many people in the world who have been labeled all kinds of names, from anti-social, people hater, unfriendly, uncooperative to name but a few only because of their personality types. If, for example, one is an introverted person, the way they behave will certainly be very different from the way an extroverted person will behave. An introverted person naturally prefers his or her own company and solitary situations over spending time with friends. An introvert will not enjoy spending too much time at a party even if the party is at his or her own home, this situation drains him or her of energy and he or she will need time to re-energize. If for instance, you were observing such a subject without knowing about this personality type or knowing the way he or she is, you might be forced to conclude the subject does not like people, which is wrong because she/ he might like people, but what she/ he does not like is spending too much time with them; and this is not of her or his choosing, it is natural.

Immediate environment – This has the potential to change the way someone appears to onlookers. A very simple example would be that if you see someone always wearing a jacket, jersey or something as protection against the cold, when you believe the weather is actually warm, you might end up concluding the person is weak of health, right? What if that person is coming from a rather hot climate and is yet to adjust to the cold she/he is currently in, wouldn't that throw your analysis into the bin? Therefore, analyzing a person take note of their immediate environment and find out if there is nothing therein that might make them change their ways. I have known a good number of people who change because they want to impress someone only to show their true personality.

The above facts show us that people can be acclimatized to respond in a certain way depending on what the prize is. There are a thousand and one things that most of us can swear they'll never do, but when something radical happens, we make an about-turn. Therefore, you have to be sure that you do not mistake adaptation as the genuine thing. If someone is forced by circumstances to do something, that does not mean they turn into what the circumstances forced them to be, because once they are clear of the undesirable circumstances, they are back into who they really are, good or bad.

Human analysis deals with psychological behavior, therefore, if you want to hold the scales even, you shall consider all aspects of psychology which may boost or pull back your investigations. There is no round way about it. Understand these concepts and utilize them as you should and your analyses will be right on the straight most of the time.

Chapter 3: Taking Advantage of the First Impression Created

First impressions last, and that is the truth. Most of what we retain about the people we meet is something we picked up the first time we met them. The same applies to you. If you have to analyze someone effectively, be sure to take special note of the first impression they created. Here is what to watch out for:

Dressing

Someone's dressing can be a giveaway but like most things about people, never take it in isolation. In general, however, it is essential to consider how much care a person takes to get dressed and even the type of dressing they prefer. If someone takes enough time to get dressed, it can either mean they prefer the confidence that looking and dressing well gives them, because we all know that looking good and confidence normally walk hand in glove. In the same line, however, never you forget that attempt can actually be a way to try and fool the world into believing that the person in question is confident, yet it is actually a bid for them to hide their lack of self-assurance.

Choice of words

The words we utter have a way of telling others a lot about us. The same words can tell others about where we have been and what we have been doing in addition to who we have been with. It is very easy to tell if a child has been spending time with some bad company from the vocabulary they suddenly develop.

The language we hear finds its way into our own words, so, as an analyst, listen to the words your subject will use and you will get to know a lot about the company they keep. Someone who grew up in a family where swearing was taboo will find it difficult to swear easily.

Tone of voice

Normally people want to be perceived in a particular way and they go all out to try and make others think of them along those lines. Someone who wants the world to perceive him as tough would speak in a tone of voice to indicate it, e.g. in a gruff voice. Have a keen ear for one's tone of voice if you are to analyze them correctly. Besides, you should also be in a position to tell the person behind the perception they want to create. People who are not so sure of themselves may actually want to be perceived as strong and use a tone of voice which depicts strength, yet they are anything but strong.

Punctuality

Whether or not someone arrives on time for an appointment speaks volumes about the type of person they are. The world is full of busy people and normally someone who does not want other people to arrive late for an appointment will try not to be late, as they would not want to disappoint someone the same way. Punctuality therefore not only shows that someone is time conscious, but can additionally show that the person knows the importance of not keeping others waiting.

Body language

Whether we like it or not, know it or not, our bodies can speak a language of their own and it would be to our best advantage to know exactly the language our bodies are speaking. For someone trying to analyze people it is even better to know and understand body language, because you will find your subjects' body language telling you more than what their lips would be saying. Folding arms, crossing legs, tapping feet all speak of something going on in the other person's head and if you can interpret these actions, you have a wealth of knowledge.

Where is the focus?

Anyone who talks about himself non-stop is too self-absorbed. As people, we should practice maintaining balance in a discussion when we meet someone for the first time. Is that what your subject is doing, or at least trying? If he/she is trying to milk you, it might mean that he/she lacks confidence and would, therefore, prefer talking about you so that attention is not drawn to him/ her.

Are they good listeners?

Don't be fooled into believing that someone's attention is fully focused on you only because they are looking at you. Listen to how the other person works at keeping the conversation going and also keep a keen ear to the way they react to your comments. Are the reactions appropriate or completely off as in the case of someone caught unawares?

Use of humor

Humor is normally good and can keep conversations flowing smoothly. However, if one has to make jokes at initial stages of association, they should be jokes which will not be misconstrued or which some people might find offensive. It is unfortunate that jokes can be cultural and a good joke you make might sound personal to someone. So, be on the lookout for the types of jokes your subject makes. Are they culturally sensitive or do they just joke away as if they have known you for ages?

Your own instinct

More often than not, your instincts are right. You might find yourself in a situation where you just do not trust someone regardless of their impeccable behavior. You find that you cannot pinpoint why exactly you feel that way, but the feeling still persists. In most cases, ignoring this feeling will lead to later regrets when you eventually discover that the person had an ace up their sleeve. If you meet a person for the first time and your instincts clearly tell you something about the person, do not brush those feelings away. Even if at close look it appears there is nothing to justify your feelings. Our feelings are closest to our spiritual self that reveals itself, and for those who believe in the spiritual world the reaction is caused by the interaction between your spirit and the other person's, so your spirit knows. I cannot rightly say anything for or against this, but it does make some sense. Why else are our instincts right most of the time?

Following the above points faithfully should lead you into making a correct analysis of the person in question. What, in your opinion, do they look like at first sight? Are they comfortable in their own skin or do they seem like they would rather be in someone else's? What feelings do you get about them the first time you meet? Use all about them at that first moment of contact as you can. You never know where your best cues will come from.

Chapter 4: Secrets and tips for non-verbal communication

There are very few things in this world which are as valuable to a would-be-analyst as the ability to discern non-verbal communication. This is because, in most instances, non-verbal communication occurs in spite of the communicator. The face or any other part of the body has its own way of communicating which the speaker might or might not be immediately aware of.

There are times when someone is struggling to hide their feeling, but our faces are such clear indicators that the emotions going on in our minds, for those who can tread the signs, can easily tell how someone is feeling. As someone trying to analyze people you should be good at it by all means. Unless someone is trying to deliberately mislead you, their facial expressions would normally have a story to tell and you'd better be ready to listen to the story.

In most cases when you ask someone why their body language was like this or like that, they do not know because it happens sub-consciously, which is what makes it the best way to analyze your subject. From a different angle, someone's actions can also say a lot about them. Someone who is naturally caring will indicate that through his or her actions. Do they help pick up what someone has dropped? Do they keep the door open for someone behind them to enter? Do they give room for someone to pass in a crowded pavement? Those are cues which rarely, if ever, lie.

In the other chapters of the books, I talked about other types of body language, but when it comes to the face it is one of the most expressive. Almost every part of the face says something, training yourself on the tips and secrets which make our faces do what they do will make you one of the best analysts around. The corner of someone's lips does not turn up or down for no reason. The brows do not suddenly shoot up or down for nothing and someone does not wet their lips when there is nothing happening in their mind. Get to know what causes even the tiniest reaction and you become unstoppable in your chosen endeavor. Here are a few you have to be able to discern.

a) **Instrumental facial actions** are those facial indicators believed to satisfy a need in the body or to manage some emotion or other within your mind. These are the most natural facial expressions as they are not learned but inborn. A grimace or a smile among other instrumental facial features like pulling up one's lower lip when disappointed are also exhibited by people blind from birth, to prove these are inborn. When someone narrows their eyes at someone, it is normally taken to mean they are displaying anger and widened eyes are normally taken to imply extreme joy or surprise. Anxiety is also believed to be shown when someone licks their lips or merely wets them.

b) **Symbolic facial actions** are those actions which we do because we learned them. These are normally shared within a culture even though there are many which are now universal. Sticking out one's tongue cannot be misconstrued for the defiance signal that it actually is just as much as pursing one's lips cannot be taken as anything other than disapproval. You can raise your eyebrows in question whether it is a direct question to what someone has said or indirect rhetorical question, where you are wondering about one thing or the other. Besides facial, some symbolic actions include victory signs, shrugging, nodding or shaking one's head which has also gained worldly meaning.

c)   **Conversational facial actions** are those normally used to highlight speech e.g. when someone says something and you open eyes wide and pucker your lips in a bid to encourage conversation and more information. Conversational facial actions are the easiest to fake and are commonly used for such means. As someone with an objective to analyze human behavior, you should be able to easily identify these actions so that you determine how genuine they are. People can easily use them depending on what they think you want to see and therefore, you are not supposed to fully depend on them. They are very misleading because they are deliberately used.

Besides the above mentioned, there are also cues people can give about the emotions they are currently going through. They are called emotion-based feelings and if you are observant enough to notice these, your analysis of human behavior will take a huge boost.

These are:

a) Macro expressions are those expressions which we make use of daily when we interact with others. They are believed to last anything from half a second to four seconds. They appear as a result of the emotions we feel as we converse with others and in most cases these are no other than fleeting emotions.

b) Micro expressions which, lasting less than half a second, are even trickier to notice than the macro expressions. Micro expressions are believed to result when a person is trying to suppress his emotions and this suppression can either be deliberate or unconscious, but the facial reaction will still be the same. Their difficulty in discerning lies in the speed with which they come and fade.

c)   Subtle emotions are believed to occur at the time when a person starts feeling the emotion which means they have not yet had time to deepen them. They are also believed to appear when someone's emotional response to whatever they are faced with is not very intense. So, unlike macro and micro, these have their basis not on how fast or slow the emotions flash through the face of your subject, but how intense (or not) they are.

Tips on implementing the above

Observation is your greatest weapon. Observe all the non-verbal cues displayed, then find out which ones you can focus on depending on which are easily faked and which ones come more naturally.

Be discerning enough to enable yourself to find out easily which facial cues are coming from sincerity and which ones might be for the benefit of those watching. This is one very useful skill any human behavior analyst should have.

Be versatile enough not to get fixated on a particular cue. For all you know, you could be the one thing that keeps you from making the right conclusion. Consider several cues together and base on that, it's more reliable.

Test the impact upon your subject. You do this by checking the intensity of their response to whatever they have been exposed to. Unfortunately, you cannot implement this tip on someone you are observing from a distance, but someone you are directly talking to.

Consider the context of the expression. Are there any external reasons why the person has reacted this way, even though he would not do the same under normal circumstances? If, for example, you expect someone to be grieving over something, then someone cracks an irresistible joke, if you are not paying attention to the context, you might be fooled into thinking they are not grieving as much as they should. In this sense, therefore, the context has the power to drag you into the wrong conclusions.

As you can see, there are many things you can find or miss merely from working on the face of your subject; the clue lies in correctly using what you have found.

Chapter 5: Body Language to instantly tell you about someone's feelings

In the previous chapter, we talked about how the face can tell you a lot more about what is going on in someone's mind. This is important because bodies speak languages very essential to your becoming a masterful analyst. The reason, as indicated earlier, is that our bodies have their own way of revealing what's inside and in most of the times the owner of the body is not aware of what the body is letting in on. Of course, there are those who have learned the art of misleading so much that they can manipulate their bodies' language to fool those looking into believing it's the genuine thing, but one has to be good at acting, otherwise the deception of the act will be known. There are many of these signs from the body, but here I will deal with the most common.

The messages your body communicates to the world

1. A genuine smile, also called the Duchene smile is determined by three main things. There are facial muscles which push upwards when someone smiles genuinely, and these cause the eyes to partially close. Those same muscles result in the creation of what are called crow's feet at the sides of one's eyes. Finally, as a result of the pushing upward of your facial muscles, the lower lip closes off the bottom teeth, fully. It is generally believed that if none of these are evident, chances are greater that the smile you are looking at is a fake one. Be on the lookout however, there are those who can practice the Duchene smile enough to master it without genuineness.

2. A shoulder shrug is a common sign of lack of knowledge, or lack of understanding. When asked a question you know no answer to, the shoulder goes up and down before the mouth has a chance to speak.

3. Crossed arms when there is warm weather are normally taken to indicate that one is closing oneself up, being defensive. It is considered an unconscious way of showing the other person that you will not let them get far with you.

4. Gravity defying movements, whether of the whole body or some part of the body, are taken to imply excitement and this is one of the most universal indicators for joy you will find. Think of throwing arms in the air or jumping into the air. Even without words you see someone doing this, you deduce that they are happy about something.

5. Gravity non-defying movements, like drooping shoulders, lowered chin, face or head and even down cast eyes indicate lack of excitement, sorrow or sadness. It is regarded as a sign of

showing defeat. Whatever is down is showing surrender.

6. Open palms are regarded as a peace offering, because they indicate that one has nothing in their hands, otherwise, the person is unarmed. They are additionally seen as a sign of honesty, truthfulness, submission and allegiance.

7. Placing your hands in front of you with palms touching is an indication of respect. The main groups to practice this are Christians as they show respect to their God, and also some Asian cultures showing respect to their masters (someone teaching them or someone with a higher position).

8. Fidgeting with your hands might indicate that you are nervous or uninterested or even irked. It might also mean you are lost (mentally) and are not sure about what exactly you should do. Playing with the hands takes your mind of what's happening. Unfortunately, it can also be considered as a sign that one is lying.

9. Tapping toes is normally taken as a clear indication that one would rather be somewhere else, or impatient, and can be taken to mean "I am anxious to be out of here". It is especially considered rude and quite unacceptable in some situations.

10. Normally when one has a sagging body, this implies seeking sympathy from whoever is looking. This sympathy seeking is normally not deliberate and bodies sag even when someone feels sorry for themselves and there is no one else watching.

11. Twinkling eyes are considered as welcoming, and they tend to put others at ease. There are those with naturally twinkling eyes and these people are normally considered as persons the others can easily feel comfortable with.

12. A pointed index finger in a closed fist indicates dominance. Most people flare up when pointed at, because they are refusing to be dominated. That finger normally and easily shoots up when someone is angry and in some cases at someone

you can't possibly dominate; but it is all in the mind. However, if it's adult to adult, it is normally unacceptable and mostly regarded as being socially unaware.

13. Sudden lowered voices indicate conspiracy. Ever seen how people strain to listen in on lowered voices, even if they were not interested when the voices were louder? This is because the belief is that if people have nothing to hide from anyone, then their voices maintain a normal pitch.

14. Some people raise voices to indicate interest in the discussion they are having and some can raise voices as an indication of anger, and this mainly depends on the how high the level is. Some people also raise voices or scream in excitement and when something extremely good happens unexpectedly.

15. Shakiness, be it a part of the body or your voice, can indicate nervousness, stress or fear. It is a way of what's inside, for instance your nervousness, showing on the outside in the

form of a shaky voice or shaking hands. Shakiness as a result of nervousness lasts for a short while, while that of fear might last the duration of the threat and even thereafter.

16. Mirroring body language can indicate companionship, or that the discussion at hand is going on well. If it's two people who are going out, and their bodies start mirroring, this can be a signal that they are headed for a great relationship because the bodies are in a bond of their own.

17. Raised eyebrows can indicate discomfort with a place, company or discussion. If someone commends you with raised eyebrows, you can take it to mean their compliment is far from being sincere. But at the same time, they can also indicate that someone is questioning the genuineness of something, especially a comment.

18. Eye contact is tricky and subject to cultural interpretation. In some cultures, it can mean disrespect, while in some it can mean sincerity,

truthfulness or honesty in some. There are also cultures where looking into someone's eyes for too long might be taken as a suggestion you have something to hide and are eye-balling to avoid shifty eyes.

19. Generally, cowering might mean you are afraid, intimidated, you lack confidence or are uncomfortable. If, on the other hand, someone is not feeling physically well, their body can become hunched in a cower-like position. Before you deduce that they are afraid, intimidated etc., find out if it is not through a physical issue.

20. Sitting back and relaxing is interpreted as a show of confidence and feeling at ease with the present company or situation. Unless you are running the show or you are in your own territory, you are discouraged sitting back and relaxing too much as this can also be misconstrued for arrogance.

21. A strong stride and steady gait is construed to mean you are confident and eager for what's

ahead, and the reverse is true; slouching is taken to mean you are fearful or do not look forward to what is lying ahead.

22. Bowing is considered a social symbol to show respect and reverence. Two people can equally bow to each other or one can bow to another. Bowing is however not equally common in all parts of the world.

23. Crossed arms with clenched fists are indicative of stubbornness or not giving in. This is also considered as a non-empathetic gesture and that you are not on the same page. A common gesture with teenage boys and preteens of both sexes.

24. Placing one's hand on the left side of the chest is considered to imply sincerity. This is however one very meaningless gesture as anyone can do it with no genuine feeling and it takes no skill not practice.

25. Thumbs up or down is a symbol that is now almost universal and has even cropped up in verbal communications. You hear people

talking of being given a 'thumbs up' to mean it was approved. It is mostly common in the Western world but the entire world is picking up on it. It is a very positive sign and should be taken to mean that there is no problem or that you can go ahead. Thumbs down is the exact opposite. You can use one or both hands but the meaning stands.

The list of the non-verbal cues is very extensive and would actually require a book to cover fully and even then, covering everything extensively would be difficult as new cues come into existence every day and internalizing them requires time, but if you are intent on being one of the best at what you want to do, it is well worth attempting it. Body language is a must to know for humans but especially for analysts.

Chapter 6: Other Cues to Consider in Analyzing People

Besides the aforementioned psychological considerations, there are more clues which you can use to analyze people. As with most of the leads you can use in your analyses, these need to be taken with a pinch of salt. In other words, be as logical as you possibly can be in your deductions about them. Remember all already mentioned considerations in your applications. Furthermore, you can use the following:

As I mentioned in a previous chapter, **Dressing** can be a huge pointer to who a person is or who a person is trying to be. Regrettably, dressing is one aspect of human lives which can be easily misconstrued. People can interpret the same thing in very different ways and this is where you as the analyst should always maintain objectivity. Let's take for instance a woman wearing a very short-skirt. If you do not put your focus entirely on the person wearing the skirt, you might be tempted to put your own thoughts into it, for example, you might end up thinking, "She is loose" someone else thinks, "She is fashionable" and if it's in an area where such dressing is not considered in good light though legal, someone might think, "She is indifferent". Whether or not these observations are true might not be as clear as we would wish it were. She might actually be wearing that skirt because she had nothing else better. How then does one conclude which of these is correct? It is achievable through not looking at this concept in isolation, but weighing it up in relation to other things as well, for example, if she is wearing it because she had nothing else, she will then be self-conscious and be trying to pull it down a little. Someone indifferent or fashionable would certainly not react that way. Be rational in your evaluation.

Someone's **Life Outlook** can also lead you into making a correct analysis about them. Life is neither all black nor all white but somewhere more central. If your subject is one person who sees nothing positive or nothing negative in life, then there is a problem somewhere. It is more natural and normal to see some positives here, negatives there and some points in between at times. Such is life. Be on the lookout for such behaviors as they can be a pointer to deeper things. There are those people who never accept someone's good deeds as just good deeds. Someone with such an outlook may have serious trust issues because of something in their past. It is more reasonable to accept that there are both honest and dishonest people in the world, and if you are one who sees no honesty wherever you look or even see honesty everywhere you look, then there are underlying points which have to be dealt with. Someone who sees dishonesty in every wall might have been misled many times in the past, and the one who sees honesty in everyone might just be simple-minded about people.

Someone's **interests** can drive you in the right way concerning your subject's character, behavior, or that which you want to know. An introvert would rather not spend time socializing at a party or such ceremonies, doing this might imply it can't be helped. Such events actually drain introverts of energy and so they try as much as they can to avoid them. In the same manner, an extrovert would not willingly spend hours alone, head buried in a book or even just thinking. Extroverts get lonely when there are no other people around, introverts prefer to be alone. An extrovert would do a lot to find company; an introvert would do a lot to avoid the company. Given a choice, what would your subject of analysis rather do? Go to a soccer match or rent a movie? A look at the person's pastime at the slightest provocation will tell you a lot. Some people enjoy life in the fast lane, and this shows in their interests.

Another signal of how a person's character could be like is the person's **associations**. Analyzing a person can include a study of the people someone associated with, when they associate, and for how long they spend time together. It is very rare, if not downright impossible, for a person to spend hours in the company of someone whose actions and words they do not like or enjoy, unless if forced into the situation. If it's free will, and you see them together several times, then it is highly likely there is a connection. The connection might not be an obvious one, but it would be there. Check for the visual cues they are displaying as they associate and you will find out whether the association is free will or forced and this will help you reach the correct conclusion.

Appearance might show you something of a person's character if used with other aspects to make a reasonable conclusion. Some people go as far as to say, "You can tell the state of someone's mind by their appearance". How many times have you heard that you need to look smart to be impressive if you are going for an interview for instance? Mostly people lie to each other that appearance does not matter that much, but life experiences show that appearance does matter because it reveals a lot about someone. It might not reveal how clever or wise or even dumb you are, but it can certainly show what you would do with the intellectual knowledge you have. It is unfortunate that when it comes to appearance that is where most would-be 'people-analysts' get it wrong, because they tend to miss a lot of details as they are looking at those things clear for everybody, even the blind. You need to watch out for minute details in appearance, those which no untrained eye would notice or care for because you are now a trained eye. Be meticulous.

Analyzing a person is not a straight forward endeavor because humans are not straight forward beings most of the time. There are networks of small things which need to be looked at in different ways. These can either lead you into the right way or get you lost. In order to be good in what you have chosen to be you need to be competent at joining many seemly unconnected things, then be reasonable in your interpretations of what you see or even do not see. Sometimes silence does speak louder that shouting and answers might actually be found where there is nothing to show.

Chapter 7: How to control and manage people through their emotions

Using other people's emotions to achieve an end can be negative or positive, but as long as you know you want to use their emotions for good then you should be able to use the information in this chapter to shift the attitudes of those you are analyzing, making sure not to use abusive manipulation which is negative no matter from which angle you may look at it. It is, therefore, imperative that you understand exactly how to achieve your desired goal without willfully doing something which will end up hurting someone. Remember emotional manipulation can have adverse effects. What is your objective?

To be able to manage someone through using their emotions you have to find out what their motivation, no matter what they do, is. Remember I mentioned earlier that with enough motivation most people would end up doing something contrary to their very nature? Try to listen, ask and look for someone to find out what makes them tick before you try to control their actions. You might actually find yourself leaning over to their ways of thought. If you fully understand their stance and it doesn't change you, you are on the best path to move them to your way of thinking. If you can influence whatever is motivating them, there is likely not going to be room for you to fail in achieving what you aim to achieve. Find out what their values are when they make decisions, get to know how they reacted to past issues like the one you are looking in on and you should be good to go.

In your desire to analyze them you might have reached the conclusion that the best way to achieving your goal is being able to control them. It is, therefore, best for you to find out what it is that holds them back enough to prevent you from getting what you are after. There is possible a stance on them which prevents them from seeing eye to eye with you. Ask them outright why they cannot see your viewpoint. If their viewpoint is not a very strong one, they might even fail to enunciate it clearly enough and, as a result, they might end up realizing they were holding on to ideas which are not worthy enough.

You have to be able to create rapport between you and them in order for you to gain their confidence. Give the room for them to become a hero in the story you are weaving around them. Show them that with them in your creation they become much better than they are outside it. Show them that your story is good, but it will never be as good if they are not a part of it. Let them feel their importance to you. Show them you cannot achieve the ultimate without them because they have a specific part to play within it. If possible, go on and show what exact part you have in mind for them.

We all align ourselves to someone who does things for us as this makes us feel that we matter. Try to the best of your ability to be helpful to them and, as a result, make them feel they are indebted to you. If you make someone feel like this, it becomes difficult for them to refuse what you ask of them, but the key lies in you being sincere in doing stuff for them. Avoid exploitation.

When people give up their beliefs for something they have been convinced to believe in, in most cases they only do that after the convincer shows them that he/she is in total control of the situation. As people, we prefer associating with someone we believe is capable of holding a situation intact enough that there will be no surprises awaiting us. Don't we all hate surprises? They have to consider you as the safe option, otherwise you won't win them over. Show them that you know what you are talking about and be confident.

To gain control over someone you should refrain from trying to act as if you are above them. Don't be judgmental, demeaning, critical, rude or confrontational. You do that and you lose, because someone can only put their trust in you if you appear to be their equal.

These points work very well, but you should never lose the objective of your endeavor, you are only doing this in a bid to get to the root of what you desire, no more and no less.

Conclusion

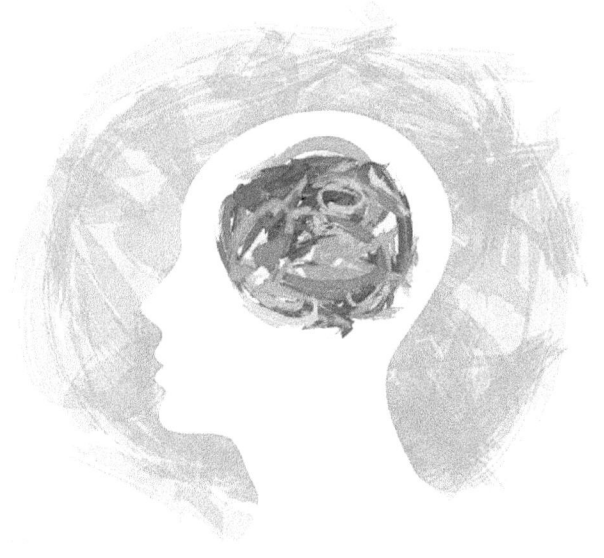

The art of analyzing people is, as you have most likely realized, not something that you can learn and master in a day. It is quite complex and if you are hell bent on achieving it, you have to be keen to take as much time as you can practice it and perfecting it. It might take you time, but it is a worthwhile endeavor and something that you will enjoy doing. It is also a practice that you never stop developing in yourself. You might use all of the provided information, but you will still learn a lot as you go on.

If, however, you got to this part of the book without cheating, then I can confidently say you might not be able to implement it yet, but you have learned a lot about analyzing people. Moreover, I can tell you, if you use all the information provided and the tips given, and use them effectively, you are well on your way to becoming a good analyst of human behavior and actions.

In the book, you read about the methods of analyzing people, how first impressions can be used to the analyst's advantage, the diverse body language people use unknowingly among others. The information herein does not, by any means, cover all there is to cover. There is still a lot more information out there which you should eat, drink and sleep with. In addition, remember you are working with the human mind and the human mind has not been studied to the full, so, more info is still coming up. Keep up to date with the coming trends and you will be one of the best human behavior analysts to grace the world. Wish you all the best in your endeavors.